Comfort
in
Sorrow

R. M. McCHEYNE

S

© Christian Focus Publications

ISBN 1 85792 012 0

This edition published in 2002 by
Christian Focus Publications Ltd,
Geanies House, Fearn, Ross-shire,
IV20 1TW, Great Britain

Extracted from
'From The Preachers Heart', 2001
ISBN 1 85792 025 2

Printed by
Cox and Wyman, Reading, Berkshire

Cover design by Alister MacInnes

Contents

1. John 11:1-4 5

2. John 11:5-10 27

3. John 11:11-16 49

4. John 11:17-27 71

5. John 11:28-35 93

6. John 11: 35-42 109

7. John 11: 43-46 125

ONE

John 11:1-4

Now a certain man was sick named Lazarus, of Bethany, the town of Mary and her sister Martha. (It was that Mary which anointed the Lord with ointment, and wiped his feet with her hair, whose brother Lazarus was sick.) Therefore his sisters sent unto him, saying, Lord, behold, he whom thou lovest is sick. When Jesus heard that, he said, This sickness is not unto death, but for the glory of God, that the Son of God might be glorified thereby.

'Man is born to trouble, as the

sparks fly upward.' Sickness goes round – it spares no family, rich or poor. Sometimes the young, sometimes the old, sometimes those in the strength of their days, are laid down on the bed of sickness. 'Remember those that suffer adversity, as being yourselves also in the body.'

The reason why God sends sickness are very varied.

1. In some it is sent for the conversion of the soul. Sometimes in health the word does not touch the heart. The world is all. Its gaieties, its pleasures, its admiration, captivate your mind. God sometimes draws you aside into a sick-bed, and shows you the sin of your heart, the vanity of worldly

pleasures, and drives the soul to seek a sure resting-place for eternity in Christ. O happy sickness, that draws the soul to Jesus! (Job 33; Ps. 107).

2. Sometimes it is for conversion of friends. When the Covenanters went out to battle, they kneeled down on the field and prayed and this was one of their prayers: 'Lord, take the ripe, and spare the green'. God sometimes does this in families. He cuts down the praying child, the child that was half-ridiculed, half-wondered at, that the rest may think, and turn, and pray.

3. Sometimes it is a frown of judgment. When worldly people go long on in a course of sin, against the light of the Bible and the warnings of ministers, God

sometimes frowns upon them, and they wither suddenly.

'He, that being often reproved, hardeneth his neck, shall suddenly be destroyed, and that without remedy' (Prov. 29:1).

'For this cause many are weak and sickly among you, and many sleep' (1 Cor. 11:30).

4. Another case is now before us – that of a child of God, sick, that Christ might be glorified in him.

(1) The case – the person

'A certain man was sick named Lazarus.' Lazarus was evidently a child of God, and yet Lazarus was sick. How he had come by his grace we are not told. His name is not mentioned before. If we may be allowed to guess, it seems probable that Mary was the first in the family who knew the Lord (Luke 10); then perhaps Martha left her 'much serving' to come also and sit at Jesus' feet; and both prevailed on their brother Lazarus to come also.

At all events he was a child of God. He was in a godly family. All the house were children of God – one in nature and one in grace. Happy family at Bethany, going hand in hand to glory! Yet here was the hand of sickness entered in – Lazarus was sick. He was peculiarly loved by Christ: 'he whom thou lovest'. 'Jesus loved Martha, and her sister, and Lazarus.' 'Our friend Lazarus sleepeth.' Like John, the disciple whom Jesus loved, so Jesus had a peculiar love for Lazarus. I cannot tell you why. He was a sinner, like other men; but perhaps when Jesus washed and renewed him, he gave him more of his own likeness than other believers. One thing is certain – Jesus loved him, and yet Lazarus was sick.

(a) Learn not to judge others because of affliction. Job's three friends tried to show him that he must be a hypocrite and a bad man, because God afflicted him. They did not know that God afflicts his own dear children. Lazarus was sick; and the beggar Lazarus was full of sores; and Hezekiah was sick, even unto death; and yet all were peculiarly dear to Jesus.

(b) God's children should not doubt his love when he afflicts. Christ loved Lazarus peculiarly, and yet he afflicted him very sore. A surgeon never bends his eye so tenderly upon his patient, as when he is putting in the lancet, or probing the wound to the very bottom. And so with Christ; he bends his eye most tenderly over his own at the time he is afflicting them.

Do not doubt the holy love of Jesus to your soul when he is laying a heavy hand upon you. Jesus did not love Lazarus less when he afflicted him, but rather more – even as a father correcteth a son in whom he delighteth (Prov. 3:12). A goldsmith when he casts gold into the furnace looks after it.

(2) The place
'Of Bethany, the town of Mary and her sister Martha.' Bethany is a

sweet retired village, about two miles from Jerusalem, in a ravine at the back of the Mount of Olives. It is at this day embosomed in fig-trees and almond trees and pomegranates. But it had a greater loveliness still in the eyes of Christ. It was 'the town of Mary and her sister Martha'.

Probably the worldly people in Jerusalem knew Bethany by its being the town of some rich Pharisee who had his country villa there or some luxuriant noble who called the lands after his own name. But Jesus knew it only as 'the town of Mary and her sister Martha'. Probably they lived in a humble cottage, under the shade of a fig-tree; but that cottage was dear to Christ. Often, as he came over the

Mount of Olives and drew near, the light in that cottage window gladdened his heart. Often he sat beneath their fig-tree telling them the things of the kingdom of God.

His Father loved that dwelling; for these were justified ones. And angels knew it well, for night and day they ministered there to three heirs of salvation. No wonder he called the place 'the town of Mary and her sister Martha'. That was its name in heaven.

So it is still. When worldly people think of our town, they call it the town of some rich merchant, some leading men in public matters, some great politician, who makes a dash as a friend of the people; not the town of our Marthas and Marys. Perhaps some poor garret where an eminent child of God dwells gives this town its name and interest in the presence of Jesus.

Dear believers, how great the love of Christ is to you! He knows the town where you live, the house where you dwell, the room where you pray. Often he stands at the door, often he puts in his hand at the hole of the door: 'I have graven thee on the palms of my hands: thy walls are continually before me'.

Like a bridegroom loving the place where his bride dwells, so Christ often says, There they dwell for whom I died. Learn to be like Christ in this. When a merchant looks at a map of the world, his eye turns to those places where his ships are sailing; a soldier looks to the traces of ancient battlefields and fortified towns; but a believer should be like Jesus, he should love the spots where believers dwell.

(3) The message
They 'sent unto him'
This seems to have been their very first recourse when the sickness came on – 'his sisters sent unto Jesus'. They did not think a bodily trouble beneath his notice. True, he had taught them that 'one thing was needful', and Mary had chosen that good part which could not be taken from her. Yet they knew well that Jesus did not despise the body.

They knew that he had a heart to bleed for every kind of grief; and therefore they sent to tell Jesus. This is what you should do: 'And call upon me in the day of trouble:

I will deliver thee, and thou shalt glorify me' (Ps. 50:15). Remember there is no grief too great to carry to him, and none too small: 'In every thing by prayer and supplication, with thanksgiving, make your requests known unto God.' 'Cast thy burden on the Lord.' Whatever it be, take it to Jesus. Some trust Christ with their soul, but not with their body; with their salvation, but not with their health. He loves to be sent for in our smallest troubles.

The argument: 'He whom thou lovest is sick'

If a worldly person had been sending to Christ, he would have sent a very different argument. He would have said: He who loves thee is sick. Here is one who has believed on thy name. Here is one that has confessed thee before the world, suffered reproach and scorn for thy sake. Martha and Mary knew better how to plead with Jesus. The only argument was in Jesus' breast: 'He whom thou lovest is sick.'

Jesus loved him with an electing love: freely from all eternity Jesus loved him. Jesus loved him with a drawing love: he drew him from under wrath, from serving sin. Jesus loved him with a pardoning love: he drew him to himself, and blotted out all his sin. Jesus loved him with an upholding love: 'Who could hold me up but thou?' He for whom thou died, he whom thou hast chosen, washed and kept till now, 'he whom thou lovest is sick'.

Learn thus to plead with Christ,

dear believers. Often you do not receive, because you do not ask aright: 'ye ask, and receive not because ye ask amiss, that ye may consume it upon your lusts.' Often you ask proudly, as if you were somebody; so that if Christ were to grant it, he would only be fattening your lusts. Learn to lie in the dust, and plead only his own free love. Thou hast loved me for no good thing in me:

Chosen, not for good in me;
Wakened up from wrath to flee;
Hidden in the Saviour's side;
By the Spirit sanctified.

Do not deny thy love. 'Have respect unto the work of thine own hands.'

A holy delicacy in prayer

They lay the object at his feet, and leave it there. They do not say: Come and heal him, come quickly, Lord. They know his love, they believe his wisdom. They leave the case in his hands: 'Lord, he whom thou lovest is sick.' They 'cast them down at Jesus' feet; and he healed them' (Matt. 15:30). They did not plead, but let their misery plead for them. 'Let your request be made known unto God' (Phil. 4:6). Learn that urgency in prayer does not so much consist in vehement pleading, as in vehement believing. He that believes most the love and power of Jesus will obtain most in prayer.

Indeed, the Bible does not forbid you using all arguments, and asking for express gifts, such as healing for sick friends. 'My little daughter lieth at the point of death: I pray thee, come and lay thy hands on her, that she may be healed; and she shall live' (Mark 5:23). 'Lord, I am not worthy that thou shouldest come under my roof: but speak the word only, and my servant shall be healed' (Matt. 8:8). Still there is a holy delicacy in prayer, which some believers know how to use. Like these two sisters, lay the object at his feet, saying: 'Lord, he whom thou lovest is sick'.

(4) The answer
(a) A word of promise: 'This sickness is not unto death'
This was an immediate answer to prayer. He did not come, he did not heal; but he sent them a word

enough to make them happy: 'This sickness is not unto death.' Away the messenger ran, crossed the Jordan, and before sunset perhaps he enters breathless the village of Bethany. With anxious faces the sisters run out to hear what news of Jesus. Good news! 'This sickness is not unto death.' Sweet promise! The hearts of the sisters are comforted, and no doubt they tell their joy to the dying man.

But he gets weaker and weaker; and as they look through their tears at his pale cheek, they begin almost to waver in their faith. But Jesus said it, and Jesus cannot lie: if it were not so, he would have told us, 'This sickness is not unto death.' At last Lazarus breathes his last sigh beside his weeping sisters. His eye is dim, his cheek is cold, he is dead; and yet Jesus said: 'Not unto death!' The friends assemble, to carry the body to the rocky sepulchre; and as the sisters turn away from the tomb, their faith dies, their hearts sink into utter gloom. What could he mean by saying, 'not unto death'?

Learn to trust Christ's Word, whatever sight may say. We live in dark times. Every day the clouds are becoming heavier and more lowering. The enemies of the Sabbath are raging. The enemies of the Church are becoming more desperate. The cause of Christ is everywhere threatened.

But we have a sweet word of promise: 'This sickness is not unto death'. Darker times are coming yet. The clouds will break and deluge our country soon with a flood of infidelity, and many will be like Mary, heart-broken.

Has the Lord's Word failed? No, never! 'This sickness is not unto death.' The dry bones of Israel shall live. Popery shall sink like a millstone, widowhood and loss of children shall come to her in one day. The kings of Tarshish and the isles shall bow their knee to Jesus. Jesus shall reign till all his enemies are put under his feet, and the whole world shall soon enjoy a real Sabbath.

(b) The explanation: 'But for the glory of God, that the Son of God might be glorified thereby'
Some might ask, Why, then, was Lazarus sick? The reason: 'For the

glory of God.' Christ was thereby in an eminent manner made known. First, his amazing love to his own was seen, when he wept at the grave. Second, his power to raise the dead. He was shown to be the resurrection and the life when he cried, 'Lazarus, come forth'.

Christ was far more glorified than if Lazarus had not been sick and died. So in all the sufferings of God's people. Sometimes a child of God says: Lord, what wilt thou have me to do? I will teach, preach, do great things for thee. Sometimes the answer is, Thou shalt suffer for my sake.

It shows the power of Christ's blood, when it gives peace in an hour of trouble, when it can make happy in sickness, poverty, persecution and death. Do not be surprised if you suffer, but glorify God.

It brings out graces that cannot be seen in a time of health. It is the treading of the grapes that brings out the sweet juices of the vine; so it is affliction that draws forth submission, weanedness from the world, and complete rest in God. Use afflictions while you have them.

TWO

John 11:5-10

Now Jesus loved Martha, and her sister, and Lazarus. When he had heard therefore that he was sick, he abode two days still in the same place where he was. Then after that saith he to his disciples, Let us go into Judea again. His disciples say unto him, Master, the Jews of late sought to stone thee; and goest thou thither again? Jesus answered, Are there not twelve hours in the day? If any man walk in the day, he stumbleth not, because he seeth the light of this world. But if a man walk in the night, he stumbleth, because there is no light in him.

(1) 'Jesus loved Martha, and Mary, and Lazarus'

These are the words of John
He knew what was in the heart of Christ, for the Holy Spirit taught him what to write, and he leaned upon Jesus' bosom, and knew the deepest secrets of Jesus' heart. This, then, is John's testimony: 'Jesus loved Martha, and Mary, and Lazarus.'

You remember they had sent this message to Jesus: 'He whom *thou lovest* is sick'. Some would have said, That was a presumptuous message to send. How did they know that Lazarus was really converted, that Jesus really loved him? But here you see John puts his seal upon their testimony. It was really true, and no presumption in it: 'Jesus loved Martha, and Mary, and Lazarus'.

How is it saints know when Jesus loves them? Christ has ways of telling his own love peculiar to himself: 'The secret of the Lord is with them that fear him.' How ridiculous is it to think that Christ cannot make known his love to the soul! I shall mention one way, by drawing the soul to himself: 'Yea, I have loved thee with an everlasting love: therefore with loving kindness have I drawn thee' (Jer. 31:3). 'Now when I passed by thee, and looked upon thee, behold, thy time was the time of love; and I spread my skirt over thee, and covered thy nakedness: yea, I sware unto thee, and entered into a covenant with thee, saith the Lord God, and thou becamest mine' (Ezek. 16:8). 'No man can come unto me except the Father draw him' (John 6:44).

Now when the Lord Jesus draws near to a dead, carnal sinner, and reveals to him a glimpse of his own beauty, of his face fairer than the sons of men, of his precious blood, of the room that there is under his wings; and when the soul is drawn away from its old sins, old ways, away from its deadness, darkness, and worldliness, and is persuaded to forsake all, and flow toward the Lord Jesus, then that soul is made to taste the peace of believing, and is made to know that Jesus loves him.

Thus Lazarus knew that Christ loved him. I was a worldly, careless man, I mocked at my sisters when they were so careful to entertain the Lamb of God, I often was angry with them. But one day he came and showed me such an excellence in the way of salvation by him. He drew me, and now I know that Jesus has loved me.

Do you know that Christ loves you? Have you this love-token, that he has drawn you to leave all and follow him, to leave your self-righteousness, to leave your sins, to leave your worldly companions for Christ, to let all go that interferes with Christ? Then you have a good token that he has loved you.

Jesus loved all the house

It seems highly probable that there was a great difference among the family: some of them were much more enlightened than others, some were much nearer Christ and some more like Christ, than others. Yet Jesus loved them all. It would seem that Mary was the most heavenly-minded of the family. Probably she was brought first to know and love the Lord Jesus Christ. She sat at the feet of Christ, when Martha was encumbered about much serving. She was also evidently more humbled under this trying dispensation than her sister was, for it is said: 'She fell down at his feet'. She seems also to have been filled with livelier gratitude for it was she that took a pound of ointment of spikenard, very costly, and anointed the feet of Christ, and wiped his feet with her hair. She did what she could. She seems to have been a very eminent believer, very full of love, and of a teachable, meek, quiet spirit. And yet Jesus loved them all – Jesus loved Martha, and her sister, and Lazarus. Every one that is in Christ is beloved by Christ, even weak members.

Good news for weak disciples
You are very apt to say: I am not a Paul, nor a John, nor a Mary. I fear Jesus will not care for me. But remember he loved Martha, and Mary, and Lazarus. He loves the weakest of those for whom he died. Just as a mother loves all her children, even those that are weak

and sickly; so Christ cares for those who are weak in the faith, who have many doubts and fears, who have heavy burdens and temptations.

Be like Christ in this
'Him that is weak in the faith receive ye, but not to doubtful disputations;' 'We then that are strong ought to bear the infirmities of the weak, and not to please ourselves' (Rom. 14:1; 15:1). There is much of an opposite spirit, I fear, amongst us. I fear that you love our Marys and Pauls and Johns, you highly esteem those that are evidently pillars. But can you condescend to men of low estate? Learn to stoop low, and to be gentle and kind to the feeble. Do not speak evil of them, do not make their blemishes the subject of your

common talk. Cover their faults. Assist them by counsel, and pray for them.

(2) Christ's delay
'When he had heard therefore that he was sick, he abode two days still in the same place where he was.'

Here seems a contradiction – Jesus loved them, and yet abode two days. You would have expected the very reverse; Jesus loved them, and therefore made no delay, but hastened to Bethany. This is the way with man's love. Human love will not brook delay. When you love anyone tenderly, and hear that he is sick, you run to see him, and to help him.

These were two important days in the cottage of Bethany. The messenger has returned, saying: 'This sickness is not unto death.' They knew that Jesus loved them, and loved their brother tenderly; and therefore they expected him to come every hour.

Martha, perhaps, would begin to be uneasy, saying, 'Why does he tarry? Why is he so long in coming? Can anything have kept him?' 'Do not fret,' Mary would say. 'You know that he loves Lazarus, and he loves us; and you know he is true, and he said: "This sickness is not unto death".' The dying man grew weaker, and at length breathed his last sigh into their affectionate bosoms. Both the sisters were overwhelmed: *he loved us, and yet he tarried two days*. So with the woman of Syrophenicia, he delayed helping her. Such are Christ's dealings with his own still. Although he loves, he sometimes on that very account tarries. Do not be surprised, and do not fret. Why does he delay:

(a) Because he is God
He sees the end from the beginning. Known unto him are all his works from the foundation of the world. Although absent in the body, he was present in the sick man's room at Bethany. He saw every change on his pale features, and heard every gentle sigh. Every tear that stole down the cheek of Mary he observed, put into his bottle, and wrote in his book. He saw when Lazarus died. But the future was before him also. He knew what he

would do, that the grave would yield up its dead, and that he would soon turn their weeping into songs of rejoicing. Therefore he stayed where he was, just because he was God. So, when Christ delays to help his saints now, you think this is a great mystery, you cannot explain it; but Jesus sees the end from the beginning. Be still, and know that Christ is God.

(b) To increase their faith
First of all he gave them a promise to hold by. He sent word by their messenger: 'This sickness is not unto death'. This was an easy and simple word for them to hold by; but, ah! it was sorely tried. When he got worse and worse, they clung to their promise with a trembling heart;

when he died, their faith died too. They knew not what to think. And yet Christ's word was true, and thus their faith was increased ever after. They were taught to believe the word of Christ, even when all outward circumstances were against them.

One evening Christ gave commandment on the Sea of Galilee to depart to 'the other side'; and as they sailed he fell asleep. Here was a simple word of promise to hold by in the storm. But when the storm came down, and the waves covered the ship, they cried, 'Master, save us; we perish.' And he said: 'Where is your faith?' By that trial the faith of the disciples was greatly increased ever after (Matt. 8:18-27). So it is with all trials of faith. When God gives a promise, he always tries our faith. Just as the roots of trees take firmer hold when they are contending with the wind, so faith takes a firmer hold when it struggles with adverse appearances.

(c) To make his help shine brighter
Had Christ come at the first and healed their brother, we never would have known the love that showed itself at the grave of Lazarus, we never would have known the power of the great Redeemer in raising from the grave. These bright forthshinings of the glory of Christ would have been lost to the Church and to the world. Therefore it was good that he stayed away for two days. Thus the honour of his name was

spread far and wide. The Son of God was glorified. 'This people have I formed for myself; they shall show forth my praise.' This is God's great end in all his dealings with his people – that he may be seen. For this reason he destroyed the Egyptians: 'That the Egyptians may know that I am the Lord.'

If Christ seems to tarry past the time he promised, wait for him; for he will come, and will not tarry. He has good reason for it, whether you can see it or not. And never forget that he loves, even when he tarries. He loved the Syrophenician even when he answered her not a word.

(3) Christ's determination
'After that saith he to his disciples, Let us go into Judea again.'

The time: 'After that...'

After the two days were over. Christ waits a certain time without helping his own, but no longer. Christ waits a certain time with the wicked before destroying them. He waited till the cup of the Amorites was full, before he destroyed them. He waited on the fig-tree a certain time. If it does not bear fruit, then, 'after that, thou shalt cut it down'. Oh, wicked man! you have a certain measure to fill; when that is filled, you will sink immediately into hell. When the sand has run, you will be cast away. So Christ has his set time for coming to his own: 'After two days will he revive us: in the third day he will raise us up, and we shall live in his sight' (Hos. 6:2).

First, *in conversion*: 'Humble

yourselves therefore under the mighty hand of God, that he may exalt you in due time' (1 Pet. 5:6). When God awakens a soul by the mighty power of his Spirit, he takes his own time and way of bringing the soul to peace. Often the sinner thinks it very hard that Christ should be so long of coming; often he begins to despair, and to think there is something peculiar in his case. Remember! wait on the Lord. It is good to wait for Christ.

Second, *in answering prayer*. When we ask for something agreeable to God's will, and in the name of Christ, we know that we have the petitions which we desire of him. But the time he keeps in his own power. God is very sovereign in the time of his answers. When

Martha and Mary sent their petition to Christ, he gave them an immediate promise; but the answer was not when they expected. So Christ frequently gives us the desires of our heart, though not at the peculiar time we desired, but a better time. Do not be weary in putting up prayers, say for the conversion of a friend. They may be answered when you are in the dust. Hold on to pray. He will answer in the best time. 'Be not weary in well-doing; for in due season we shall reap, if we faint not.'

Third, *in his own second glorious coming*. Christ said to the church long ago: 'Yet a little while, and he that shall come will come, and will not tarry.' And still the time is prolonged. The Bridegroom seems to tarry; but he will come at the due time. He waits for infinitely wise reasons. And the moment that he should come, the heavens shall open, and he will appear.

The objection
The objection was, that it was dangerous to him and to them, because the Jews had sought to stone him before. Another time Peter made objection to Christ, saying: 'Be it far from thee, Lord. This shall not be unto thee. But he turned and said unto Peter, Get thee behind me, Satan; thou art an offence unto me, for thou savourest not the things that be of God, but the things that be of men.' How selfish are even godly men! The disciples did not care for the distress

of Martha and Mary. They did not care for the pain of their friend Lazarus. They were afraid of being stoned, and that made them forget the case of the afflicted family. There is no root deeper in the bosom than selfishness. Watch and pray against it. Even the godly will sometimes oppose you in what is good and right. Here, when Christ proposed that they should go into Judea again, the disciples opposed it. They were astonished at such a proposal. They, as it were, reproved him for it. Think it not strange, dear brethren, if you are opposed by those who are children of God, especially if it be something in which you are called to suffer.

Christ's answer

The path of duty Christ here compares to walking in the daylight. 'If a man walk in the day, he stumbleth not.' As long as a man has got a good conscience, and the smile and the presence of God, he is like one walking in the daytime; he plants his foot firmly and boldly forward. But if a man shrink from the call of God, through fear of man, and at the call of worldly prudence, he is like one walking in darkness: 'He stumbleth, because there is no light.'

Oh, that you who are believers would be persuaded to follow Jesus fearlessly wherever he calls you! If you are a believer, you will often be tempted to shrink back. The path of a Christian is narrow, and often difficult. But what have you to fear? Have you the blood of Christ upon your conscience, and the presence of God within your soul? Are there not twelve hours in the day? Are we not all immortal till our work is done?

THREE

John 11:11-16

These things said he: and after that he saith unto them, Our friend Lazarus sleepeth; but I go, that I may awake him out of sleep. Then said his disciples, Lord, if he sleep, he shall do well. Howbeit Jesus spake of his death: but they thought that he had spoken of taking of rest in sleep. Then said Jesus unto them plainly, Lazarus is dead. And I am glad for your sakes that I was not there, to the intent ye may believe; nevertheless let us go unto him. Then said Thomas, which is called

Didymus, unto his fellow disciples,
Let us also go, that we may die with
him.

(1) Christ's love to a dead Lazarus
He calls him friend

An eminent infidel used to say that
neither patriotism nor friendship was
taught in the Bible. He only proved
that he neither knew nor understood
the Bible. How different the
sentiment of the Christian poet, who
says,

> The noblest friendship ever
> shown,
> The Saviour's history makes
> known.

Ah! it is an amazing truth that
Jehovah-Jesus came and made
friends of such worms as we are.
True friendship consists in mutual

confidence and mutual sacrifices. Thus God dealt with Enoch: 'Enoch walked with God three hundred years.' Enoch told all to God, and God told all to him. Blessed friendship between Jehovah and a worm! So God treated Abraham. Three times in the Bible he is called 'the friend of God' (2 Chron. 20:7; Isa. 41:8; Jas. 2:23). 'He raised up the righteous man from the East and called him to his foot.' The God of glory appeared unto Abraham, and we find God saying, 'Shall I hide from Abraham that thing which I do?' (Gen. 18:17). So God dealt with Moses: 'the LORD spake unto Moses face to face, as a man speaketh unto his friend.' And God said to him, 'My presence shall go with thee, and I will give thee rest'

(Exod. 33:11, 14). 'And when Moses went in before the LORD to speak with him, he took the veil off' (Exod. 34:34).

Thus did Christ deal with his disciples. Though he was the holy Lamb of God, yet he says: 'Henceforth I call you not servants; for the servant knoweth not what his lord doeth: but I have called you friends; for all things that I have heard of my Father I have made known unto you' (John 15:15). He admitted them to the closest fellowship; so that one leaned on his breast at supper, and another washed his feet with ointment. He told them freely all that he had learned in the bosom of his Father – all that they were able to bear of the Father's glory, the Father's love.

Thus he dealt with Lazarus: 'Our friend Lazarus.' Often, no doubt, they had sat beneath the spreading fig tree at the cottage of Bethany, and Christ had opened up to them the glories of an eternal world.

This is what you are invited to, dear friends – to become the friends of Jesus. When men choose friends, they generally choose the rich, or the wise, or the witty; they ask those that will invite them back. Not so with Christ. He chooses the poor, the foolish, babes, and makes them friends – those of whom the world is ashamed. *The world changes friends*. In the world, if a rich friend wax poor, if overtaken by a sudden failure, and plunged in deepest poverty, friends, like butterflies in the rain, fly quickly home; they look cold and strange, as if they did not see you. Not so Jesus, the friend that sticketh closer than a brother. A true friend does not hide anything from another which it would be good for him to know. Neither does Christ: 'Shall I hide from Abraham that thing which I do?'

Even when dead: 'Our friend Lazarus'

Few people remember the dead. They are 'a wind that passeth away, and cometh not again'; 'The place that knows them shall know them no more for ever.' In some of the countries where I have been, there are immense burying-grounds where cities have been, but where not a living being now remains.

There is not one to remember their name, or to shed a tear over their memory. Even among yourselves, how soon are the dead forgotten! Although you loved them well when living ('lovely and pleasant in their lives'), yet when they are out of sight, they are soon out of mind. But Christ's dead are never forgotten. There is one faithful Brother, who keeps in mind the sleeping dust of all of his brothers and sisters. Death makes no change in the love of Christ; death cannot separate us from his love; death does not take us off his breastplate. 'Our friend Lazarus sleepeth.'

Ah, my friends! this is how to take the sting away from death. You will, no doubt, be forgotten by the world;

if you are Christ's, they never loved you, and will be glad when you are gone. Living sermons are no pleasant objects in the world's eye. They will be glad when you are under the sod. Even believers will forget you. Man is a frail creature, and memory is fading. But Christ never will forget you. He that said, 'My faithful martyr Antipas!' when all the world had forgotten him, remembers all his sleeping saints and will bring them with him.

(2) The mistake (12, 13)
In the last lecture we had a specimen of the selfishness of the disciples – here of their stupidity. They were beloved disciples who had left all to follow Christ and sincerely believed his word and

loved his person; and yet what remains of blindness in the understanding! 'If he sleep, he shall do well.'

To *sleep* was the common expression for the death of saints in the Old Testament. Thus God said to Moses: 'Thou shalt sleep with thy fathers.' And to Daniel: 'Many of those that sleep in the dust of the earth shall awake.' To King David: 'Thou shalt sleep with thy fathers.' 'Now shall I sleep in the dust' (Job 7:21). 'Lest I sleep the sleep of death' (Ps. 13:3). Surely if they had thought a little, they might have found the meaning!

What would have been the use of going to awake him out of a refreshing sleep? Did they think so lightly of their Master, as that he would run into personal danger to awaken a sleeping man? Do not wonder when disciples mistake the meaning of Christ's words. They have done so before, and may do it again. Every gracious man is not an infallible man. Learn to search patiently into the meaning of Christ's words, by comparing Scripture with Scripture, and especially going to him for light. When you are reading in a dark room, and come to a difficult part, you take it to the window to get more light. So take your Bibles to Christ.

What was the cause of their mistake? *Fear*. They did not want to go into Judaea again. They were afraid of being stoned. They saw their Master was bent upon going, and they wanted to dissuade him.

They misunderstood his words, because of the averseness of their hearts to his will. This is the great reason of all blindness in divine things: 'Through the blindness of their hearts'; 'If any man will do the will of God, he shall know of the doctrine.'

The reason why many of you do not understand your lost condition, is not that it is not taught in the Bible, not that the words are difficult (the Bible is a plain, simple book) but it is that you do not wish to be convinced of sin; you do not want your fine dreams of your own goodness and safety to be dashed to pieces. The reason why many of you do not understand the way of forgiveness is that you do not like it. Your heart is averse from God's way, you cannot bear to have all your righteousness accounted rags, and to be beholden entirely to the righteousness of Jesus. The reason why many saints among you cannot see your rule of duty plain, is that you are averse from the duty. You want to have your own way, and you cannot understand the Scriptures that contradict it. This was the case with the apostles. This is frequently the case in entering into marriage, or a servant fixing on a place. When once a strong desire is formed in the heart, it blinds the mind to the Scriptures.

Pray for a pure heart, that you may be filled with the knowledge of his will, that you may walk worthy of the Lord to all pleasing!

(3) The explanation (14, 15)

Christ here explains two things: his words and his absence.

Jesus said plainly, 'Lazarus is dead!' His disciples had shown great selfishness, great blindness of heart, great stupidity, and yet he was not angry, neither did he turn away. But he said plainly, 'Lazarus is dead.' When he had been teaching them many things, he said, 'Have ye understood all these things?' (Matt. 13:51). Another time, when he had been telling them of the Father's house, Thomas said: 'Lord, we know not whither thou goest.' With the same admirable patience and gentleness he said: 'I am the way, and the truth, and the life: no man cometh unto the Father, but by me.' He 'can have compassion on the ignorant, and on them that are out of the way.' Perhaps some of you feel dead and ignorant – you need not keep away from Christ on that account. Take your blind eyes to him, that he may give you sight. He wants you to understand his way and his will.

He explains his absence: 'I am glad I was not there'
The objection would immediately arise in the breast of his disciples, If Lazarus be dead, why did our Master stay these two days? Therefore he explains that it was for their sakes. Had Christ been there, he felt that he must have healed Lazarus. Had he been there, Lazarus had not died.

Christ could not have stood in the cottage of Bethany, and looked on the face of his dying friend, and seen the silent tears of Mary, and heard the imploring words of Martha without granting their desire. Therefore he says: 'I am glad I was not there.' Ah! learn the amazing love of Christ to his own. He cannot deny their prayer. When Moses was pleading with God, God said: 'Let me alone.' God could not destroy Israel so long as Moses pleaded for them. So God had to tell Jeremiah, 'Pray not for this people.' And so when God wants to destroy, he shuts up his saints that they cannot pray. Jesus kept away, that he might not be overcome by their prayer. The uplifted hand of a believing Mary is too much for Jesus to resist. The tearful eye of an earnest believer is 'terrible as an army with banners'. 'Turn away thine eye from me, for thou hast overcome me.' But why was he not there? 'For your sakes, to the intent ye may believe.'

In the last lecture, we saw he delayed for the sake of the cottagers at Bethany; here is another reason – 'For your sakes.'

'All things are for your sakes' (2 Cor. 4:15). For the sake of believers this world was created – the sun made to rule the day, and the moon to rule the night; every shining star was made for them. All are kept in being for your sakes. Winds rise and fall, waves roar and are still, seasons revolve, seed-time and harvest, day and night – all for your sakes. 'All things are yours.'

All events are for your sakes. Kingdoms rise and fall to save God's people. Nations are his rod, his saw and axe to hew out a way for the chariot of the everlasting gospel; even as Hiram's hewers in Lebanon and the Gibeonite drawers of water were building up the temple of God. The enemies of the church are only a rod in God's hand. He will do his purpose with them, then break the rod in two, and cast it away.

Specially all the providences of believing families are for your sakes. When Christ is dealing with a believing family, you say, That is no matter of mine. What have I to do with it? Ah, truly if you are of the world, you have no part or lot in it! But if you are Christ's, it is for your sake, to the intent that ye may believe. The dealings of Christ with believing families are very instructive, his afflictions and his comforts, his way.

O learn to bear one another's burdens, to see more of Christ's hand among you, to the intent that ye may believe!

There's not a plant that grows below
But makes his glory known;
And thunders roll and tempests blow
By order from the throne.

(4) The zealous disciple
'Let us also go, that we may die with him.' What voice is that? It is Thomas, unbelieving Thomas.
There is true love to Christ here.

He saw that Christ was determined to go; he saw the danger, he counted the cost. Well, says he, 'Let us go also.' Strange, that following the Lamb of God should endanger our very life; yet in how many ages of the Church it has been so! 'The time will come when whosoever killeth you, shall think that he doeth God service.' What a cloud of witnesses has Scotland seen, all saying, like Thomas, 'Let us go and die with him!' Ah, we do not know the value of Christ, if we will not cleave to him unto death!

True zeal toward others: 'Let us go.' He does not say, like Peter, 'I am ready to go with thee'; but, 'Let *us* go.' Whenever we clearly apprehend the path of duty, we should persuade others to come along with us. It is not enough for a believer to go in the way himself; you must say, 'Let us go.' So Israel: 'Come, and let *us* join ourselves to the LORD' (Jer. 50:5). So Moses to Hobab: 'Come thou with *us*.' So the converted Gentiles: 'O house of Israel, come ye and let *us* walk in the light of the Lord.' A Christian should be like a river that fertilizes while it runs, carrying ships and all that floats upon its bosom, along with it to the ocean.

Yet there is sin mingled with it. Jesus spoke not of dying; on the contrary, he spoke of 'not stumbling'. But Thomas was full of unbelief, and full of fear. He heeded not the word of Christ. Learn how much sin and weakness mingles with our love and zeal, and what infinite need we have of one who bears the iniquity of our holy things.

FOUR

John 11:17-27

Then when Jesus came, he found that he had lain in the grave four days already. Now Bethany was nigh unto Jerusalem, about fifteen furlongs off: And many of the Jews came to Martha and Mary, to comfort them concerning their brother. Then Martha, as soon as she heard that Jesus was coming, went and met him: but Mary sat still in the house. Then said Martha unto Jesus, Lord, if thou hadst been here, my brother had not died. But I know, that even now, whatsoever thou wilt ask of God, God will give it thee. Jesus saith unto her, Thy brother shall rise again. Martha saith unto him, I know that he shall rise again in the resurrection at the last day. Jesus said unto her, I am the resurrection, and the life: he that believeth in me, though he were dead, yet shall he live: And whosoever liveth and believeth in me shall never die. Believest thou this? She saith unto him, Yea, Lord: I believe that thou are the Christ, the Son of God, which should come into the world.

(1) Christ orders all events for his own glory

One day, when Christ had healed a man deaf and dumb, the multitude cried: 'He hath done all things well.' Ah! this is true indeed of the Lord

Jesus Christ. 'He is head over all things to the church.' He that died to redeem us from hell, lives to make all things work together for our good. 'He healeth the broken in heart, and bindeth up their wounds. He telleth the number of the stars; he calleth them all by their names' (Ps. 147:3,4). The same hand that was nailed to the cross for us brings out Arcturus and the Pleiades, and guides the sun in his journey – and all for us. A striking example of this we have now before us.

In the time: 'He found that he had lain in the grave four days already' (v. 17). We saw that when he heard that Lazarus was sick, he remained two days in the same place where he was. Then slowly and calmly he left the secluded glens of Mount Gilead, and, crossing the Jordan, came on the fourth day to the village of Bethany. The shady ravines of Mount Olivet wore an aspect of gloom. The village was silent and still, and perhaps around the cottage door of Lazarus a group of mourners sat upon the ground.

Jesus and the disciples halted a little way from the village, as if unwilling to break in upon the scene of deep sorrow. At length a passing villager tells them that Lazarus is dead, and this is the fourth day he has been lying in the cold rocky tomb. The disciples looked at one another, and wondered. Four days dead! Why did our Master tarry? Why did we lose two days on the other side of Jordan? The sisters also thought Jesus came too late. 'If thou hadst been here, my brother had not died.' The Jews also wondered.

Yet Jesus came at the right time. Had he come later, the sensation would have passed away, the death of Lazarus would have been forgotten in the whirl of the world. We soon forget the dead. Had he come sooner, the death of Lazarus would not have been known. He came in due time. He orders all things for his glory – he doeth all things well.

In the place: 'Bethany was nigh unto Jerusalem' (v. 18). The place of this wonder of grace was also chosen with infinite skill. Bethany was a retired village, in a shady, secluded ravine entirely removed from the bustle and noise of the city. So that there was opportunity for Christ to exhibit those tender emotions of pity and love, weeping and groaning, which he could not have done in the bustle of a crowded city.

And yet Bethany was nigh unto Jerusalem, about fifteen furlongs, or two miles, so that many Jews were present as witnesses; and the news of it was carried in a few hours to the capital, and spread all over Jerusalem and Judaea. Had it been done in a corner, men would have derided and denied it. But it was done within half an hour's walk of Jerusalem, so that all might ascertain its reality. Christ chooses the place where he does his wonders wisely and well, all to show forth his own glorious name. He chooses the spot where to break the alabaster box, so that the ointment may be most widely diffused.

In the witnesses: 'Many of the Jews' (v. 19). From verses 45, 46 we learn that the company were far from being all friends of Christ. Perhaps they would not have come if they had known Christ was to be there. But they were friends of Martha and Mary, and though they did not like their serious ways, yet in an hour of affliction they could not but visit them to give them such comfort as they were able. This is the way of the world. There is much natural kindness remaining in the bosom even of worldly men. Christ knew this, and therefore chose this very time to arrive. Ah, friends, he doeth all things well. You often wonder, often murmur, at the way that he takes you.

Learn that if you are his, he will make all things work together for your good, and his own glory. Learn to trust him, then, in the dark, in the darkest frowns of providence, in the most painful delays. Learn to wait upon him. 'It is good for a man both to hope and quietly wait for the salvation of God.' He is good to the soul that waiteth for him.

(2) See here the weak believer
Jesus and his disciples had halted a little way from the village, under the shade of the trees. But word

soon came to the ear of Martha that the Saviour was come. She immediately hastened to meet him. Ah! who can tell what love and compassion must have appeared in his eye, what holy calmness on his brow, what tenderness upon his lips? He was the Rose of Sharon and the Lily of the valleys. Yet Martha is not hushed at the sight. She bursts out into this impassioned cry: 'Lord, if thou hadst been here, my brother had not died.' Observe:

Her presumption. 'If thou hadst been here, my brother had not died.' How did she know this? What promise of the Bible could she name upon which this expectation was grounded? God had promised that his own shall never want bread nor any good thing, that he will supply all their need, that they shall never perish, that he will be with them in time of trouble. But nowhere has he promised that they shall not die. On the contrary, 'Israel must die.' David prays: 'Make me to know mine end, and the measure of my days.' And Job: 'I would not live alway.'

Her limiting of Christ: 'If thou hadst been here.' Why so? Am I a God at hand, and not afar off? 'Is my hand shortened at all, and have I no power to redeem?' She forgot the centurion of Capernaum: 'Lord, I am not worthy that thou shouldest come under my roof: but speak the word only' (Matt. 8:8). She forgot the nobleman's son at Capernaum: 'Sir, come down, ere my child die ...

Go thy way, thy son liveth' (John 4:49, 50). Her grief and anguish kept her from calmly remembering the works and power of Jesus.

Her unbelief: 'But I know that even now' (v. 22). This was faith, and yet unbelief. She believed something, but not all, concerning Jesus. She believed in him as an advocate and intercessor, but not that all things were given into his hands, that he is Lord of all, head over all things to the church. Her grief and confusion and darkness hid many things from her.

And yet she came to Jesus. Though grieved, she was not offended; she did not keep away from him. She poured out all her grief, darkness and complaint into his bosom. This is just the picture of a weak believer: much of nature and little grace, many questionings of Christ's love and power, and yet carrying their complaints only to him. It was not to the Jews Martha told her grief, it was not to the disciples, it was to Jesus himself.

Learn that afflicting time is trying time. Affliction is like the furnace, it discovers the dross as well as the gold. Had all things gone on smoothly at Bethany, Martha and Mary had never known their sin and weakness; but now the furnace brought out the dross. Learn to guard against unbelief. Guard against presumption, making a Bible-promise for yourself, and leaning upon a word God has never spoken. Guard against prescribing your way to Christ, and limiting him in his dealings. Guard against unbelief, believing only part of God's testimony. 'O foolish, and slow of heart to believe all that God hath spoken.' Remember, whatever your darkness may be, to carry your complaint to Jesus himself.

(3) Jesus reveals himself (vv. 23-26)

Not a feature of Christ's face was ruffled by the passionate cry of Martha. He was not angry, and did not turn away, but opened up more of himself than he had ever done. 'Thy brother shall rise again.' He comforts her by the assurance that her brother shall rise again, and then leads her to see that all the spring and source of that is in himself. Two things he shows in himself.

First, *I am the resurrection*: 'He that believeth in me, though he were dead, yet shall he live.' Christ here reveals himself as the head of all dead believers.

He shows what he is: I am the author or spring of all resurrection. The fountain of the resurrection is in my hand. It is my voice that shall call forth the sleeping dust of all my saints. It is my hand that shall gather their dust and fashion it like my own glorious body. All this is mine. At my command Enoch was translated. I also carried away Elijah. I will raise the myriads of sleeping believers also. Believest thou this? Believest thou that he who has sat so often under thy roof and fig-tree, at thy table, that he is the resurrection?

He shows the certainty that all dead believers shall live: 'He that believeth on me, though he were dead, yet shall he live.' If I am the resurrection, then surely I will raise every one for whom I died. I will not lose one of them. Here is comfort for those of you who, like Martha, weep over the believing dead. Thy brother shall rise again. Jesus, who died for them, is the Resurrection. That great work of gathering and raising their scattered dust is committed to Jesus. 'They shall be mine, in that day when I shall make up my jewels.'

Oh, what unspeakable comfort it will be to be raised from the grave by Jesus! If it were an angel's voice we might wish to lie still; but when the voice of our Beloved calls, how gladly shall we arise!

> Sweet thought to me!
> I shall arise,
> And with these eyes
> My Saviour see.

Oh, what unspeakable terror it will give to you that are Christless, to hear the voice of Jesus breaking the long silence of the tomb!

Second, *I am the life*: 'He that liveth and believeth in me shall never die.' Christ here reveals himself as the head of all living believers.

He directs her eye to himself: 'I am the life.' This name is frequently applied to the Lord Jesus: 'In him was life; and the life was the light of men' (John 1:4); 'When Christ, who is our life, shall appear, then shall ye also appear with him in glory' (Col. 3:4); 'For the life was manifested, and we have seen it, and bear witness, and shew unto you that eternal life, which was with the Father, and was manifested unto us' (1 John 1:2). And therefore Jesus says: 'Ye will not come unto me that ye might have life.' In my hand is the source of all natural, spiritual and eternal life. Every thing that lives derives its life from me, every living soul. Every drop of living water flows from my hand. I begin, I carry on, I give eternal life.

He shows the happy consequence to all living believers. 'They shall never die.' Their life suffers no interruption by the death of the body. Death has no power to quench the vital flame in the believer's soul. If I be the life, I will keep all mine, even in the valley of the shadow of death. They shall never perish. Believest thou this? Here is comfort to those of you who, like Martha, tremble at the sight of death. Ah! it is a ghastly sight when it comes, the terror of kings and the king of terrors. There is something dreadful in the still features, the silent lips, the glazed eye, the cold hand that no more returns our fond pressure, but rather sends a chill through the blood. Ah! you say, must we all thus die? Where is the gospel now? *Answer.* Jesus is the life, the spring of eternal life to all his own. Believe this, and you will triumph over the grave.

(4) Martha's confession
When her faith flowed out. When the south wind blows softly upon a bed of spices, it causes the fragrant odours to flow out. So when Jesus breathed on this believer's heart, saying: 'I am the resurrection and the life,' it drew from her this sweet confession: 'Yea, Lord, I believe.'

This shows how faith and love spring up in the heart. Some of you seek for faith much in the same way as you would dig for a well. You turn the eye inward upon yourself and search amidst the depths of your polluted heart to find if faith is there; you search amid all your feelings at sermons and sacraments to see if faith is there; and still you find nothing but sin and disappointment.

Learn Martha's plan. She looked full in the face of Jesus; she saw his dust-soiled feet and sullied garment, and his eye of more than human tenderness. She drank in his word: 'I am the resurrection and the life;' and in spite of all she saw and all she felt, she could not but believe. The discovery that Jesus made of his love and power, as the head of dead believers and the head of living believers, revived her fainting soul, and she cried: 'Yea, Lord, I believe.' Faith comes by hearing the voice of Jesus.

Upon what her faith flowed out: upon the person of Jesus. It seems probable that Martha did not comprehend all that was implied in the words of the Lord Jesus. Something she saw, but much she did not see. Still on this one thing her faith fastens – that Jesus is the Christ, the Son of God. So do you, brethren, when glorious promises are unfolded, whose full meaning you cannot comprehend. Embrace Jesus and you have all: 'for all the promises of God in him are yea, and in him amen, to the glory of God by us.' Much you cannot comprehend, for it doth not yet appear what we shall be; yet take a whole Christ into the arms of your faith, and say: 'Yea, Lord, I believe that thou art the Christ, the Son of God, which should come into the world.'

FIVE

John 11:28-35

And when she had so said, she went her way, and called Mary her sister secretly, saying, The Master is come, and calleth for thee. As soon as she heard that, she arose quickly, and came unto him. Now Jesus was not yet come into the town, but was in that place where Martha met him. The Jews then which were with her in the house, and comforted her, when they saw Mary, that she rose up hastily and went out, followed her, saying, She goeth unto the grave to weep there. Then when Mary was come where Jesus was, and saw him, she fell down at his feet, saying unto him, Lord, if thou hadst been here, my brother had not died. When Jesus therefore saw her weeping, and the Jews also weeping which came with her, he groaned in the spirit, and was troubled, and said, Where have ye laid him? They said unto him, Lord, come and see. Jesus wept.

(1) The calling of Mary
Martha is the messenger
Martha had got a little comfort from that sweet word of Jesus, 'I am the resurrection and the life.' Her faith had been revived by the question, 'Believest thou this?' The swelling tide of sorrow in her breast was

calmed: 'And when she had so said, she went her way, and called Mary.'

Those who have been comforted by Christ themselves are the fittest messengers to bring comfort to others: 'Blessed be God, even the Father of our Lord Jesus Christ, the Father of mercies, and the God of all comfort; who comforteth us in all our tribulation, that we may be able to comfort them which are in any trouble, by the comfort wherewith we ourselves are comforted of God' (2 Cor. 1:3, 4).

God takes his ministers through divers trials and consolations, just that he may make them fitting messengers to comfort others. O! it is then we can tell others of the excellence of the apple-tree, when we have been sitting under its shadow and eating its pleasant fruits. Martha was but a weak believer compared with Mary, and yet she is made the channel of conveying the joyful news to her. It is a great mistake to think that none but eminent believers are made useful in the church of God. God often feeds eminent believers by a weak ministry. The minister has often less grace than those to whom he ministers. Especially when eminent believers are cast down and perplexed, frequently a very small means is used to lift them up again.

She called her secretly
The last time the Saviour was in Judea, they took up stones to stone

him to death; and probably some of the Jews who were sitting beside Mary were among his bitter enemies. Martha therefore came in, and whispered softly into Mary's ear, 'The Master is come and calleth thee.' She feared the Jews. Jesus had done much for her, and she was tender of his safety and of his cause. Thus does it become those of you for whom Jesus has done much to be tender of his honour, tender of his name and cause. You will feel as a member of his body, and that you have no interest separate from him.

The message: 'The Master is come, and calleth for thee'
Mary was sitting sad and desolate in the cottage at Bethany. It was

now the fourth day from the funeral, and yet no comfort came. The place of Lazarus was empty; the house looked desolate without him, and Jesus had not come. He had sent them a message that this sickness was not unto death. Yet his word was broken, and he had not come. Mary knew not what to think. Why does he tarry beyond Jordan? She would say to herself, Has he forgotten to be gracious? Suddenly her sister whispers, 'The Master is come and calleth for thee.' Christ was near the cottage before she knew. So it was that morning at the Lake of Tiberias, when 'Jesus stood on the shore, but the disciples knew not that it was Jesus'; or that evening when the two disciples went to Emmaus and Jesus drew near, but their eyes were holden that they did not know him.

So does death come upon the believer in Jesus. 'The Master is come, and calleth for thee.' So will Jesus come to his weeping, desolate church, and this cry shall awake the dead. 'The Master is come, and calleth for thee.'

(2) Mary's going (vv. 29-31)

She arose quickly

It is evident that Mary was the more deeply affected of the two sisters. Martha was able to go about, but Mary sat still in the house. She felt the absence of Christ more than Martha. She believed his word more, and when that word seemed to fail, Mary's heart was nearly broken. Ah! it is a deep sorrow when natural and spiritual grief come together. Affliction is easily borne if we have the smile of Jehovah's countenance.

Why does the mourner rise, and hastily drying her tears, with eager step leave the cottage door? Her friends who sat around her she seems quite to forget. 'The Master is come.' Such is the presence of the Lord Jesus to mourners still. The world's comforters are all physicians of no value. Miserable comforters are they all. They have no balm for a wounded spirit. 'The heart knoweth its own bitterness.' But when the Master comes and calls us, the soul revives. There is life in his call, his voice speaks peace. 'In me ye shall have peace.' Mourners should rise up quickly, and go to Jesus. The bereaved should spread their sorrows at the feet of Christ.

The place: 'Now Jesus was not yet come into the town' (v. 30)
Jesus had probably come far that day, perhaps all the way from Jericho. He had journeyed onwards on foot, till he came to the foot of the Mount of Olives, and halted beneath the trees that skirt the village of Bethany.

He did not go into the town till he had finished the work for which he came. Perhaps he was hungry and thirsty, as he was that day when he sat beside Jacob's well, and said, 'Give me to drink.' But he did not mention it now. His mind was intent upon his work – the raising of dead

Lazarus, and the glorifying of his Father's great name. 'I have meat to eat that ye know not of.' 'My meat is to do the will of him that sent me, and to finish his work.'

Christ's delight in saving sinners, and doing good to his own, overcame his sense of hunger and thirst and weariness. Oh! see what a ready high-priest we have to go to. And see what is our true happiness, namely, to do God's holy will, not much minding bodily comforts. They have most of the mind of Christ, and most of the joy of Christ, who prefer his service to bodily rest and refreshment.

The Jews followed Mary
We saw that it was natural kindness that brought them to Bethany; and

so natural kindness makes them follow Mary now. They could not comprehend her spiritual grief, and thought she was going to the grave to weep there. Yet this was the means of leading some of them to the spot where they were born again. 'Many of the Jews believed on him.'

How wonderful are God's ways of leading men to Christ! 'And I will bring the blind by a way that they know not: I will lead them in paths that they have not known.' One soul is led by curiosity, like Zaccheus, to go and hear a particular minister, and the word is sent home with power. Another goes in kindness to a friend, and is arrested and sent home with a bleeding heart. His name is

Wonderful – his ways are wonderful, his grace is wonderful. Learn that it is good to cleave to the godly, and to go with them. They may lead you to where Jesus is.

(3) The meeting with Jesus (vv. 32-35)

Mary's tender humility

With eager footstep Mary hurried over the rocky footpath. Jesus was standing in the same place where Martha met him; and as Mary approached, he bent his compassionate eyes upon her. Mary saw, and fell at his feet. What a crowd of feelings were in her breast at that moment! She wondered why he had not come sooner. That was a dark mystery to her. She knew he was her Saviour, and the Son of God. She knew that he loved her. And yet she fell at his feet. She felt that she was a vile sinner, worthy to be trampled on. She felt that she was a worm, and that all her hope was in Jesus. Ah! brethren, it is sweet to be able to take Mary's place. The most eminent believers are the lowliest. Paul said: 'I am the chief of sinners' and 'I am less than the least of all saints.' The nearer you take anything to the light, the darker its spots appear; and the nearer you live to God, the more you will see your own utter vileness.

Mary repeats Martha's complaint: 'Lord, if thou hadst been here, my brother had not died' (v. 32)
   From this it is plain that the two

sisters had been often conversing upon Christ's absence; and they had agreed upon this, that if Christ had been there, their brother had not died. It was both presumptuous and unbelieving. Perhaps Mary learned it from Martha. We are very apt to learn unbelief from one another. The Bible says: 'Exhort one another daily, while it is called today.' But believers frequently discourage one another.

Jesus' compassion

When he saw, he groaned in the spirit, and was troubled. This is humanity. His eye affected his heart, when he saw her weeping – her whom he loved so well, so eminent a believer, one whom he had washed and justified. When he saw the Jews weeping, mere worldly friends, he groaned within himself. So when he came near, and beheld the city, he wept over it; when he saw the widow of Nain, he had compassion on her; when he saw the multitudes of Galilee, like sheep without a shepherd, he had compassion on them. All this shows his perfect humanity. He is bone of our bone, and flesh of our flesh.

He asked, Where have ye laid him? This also was human. As God he knew well where they had laid him; but he wanted them to lead him to the grave.

Jesus wept. When he saw the cave, and the stone, and the weeping friends, 'Jesus wept'. He wept because his heart was deeply touched. It was not feigned weeping, it was real. He knew that he was to raise him from the dead, and yet he wept because others wept. He wept as our example, to teach us to weep with one another. He wept to show what was in him: 'For we have not an high-priest which cannot be touched with the feeling of our infirmities; but was in all points tempted like as we are, yet without sin. Let us therefore come boldly unto the throne of grace, that we may obtain mercy, and find grace to help in time of need' (Heb. 4:15, 16).

SIX

John 11: 35-42

Jesus wept. Then said the Jews, Behold how he loved him! And some of them said, Could not this man, which opened the eyes of the blind, have caused that even this man should not have died? Jesus therefore again groaning in himself cometh to the grave. It was a cave, and a stone lay upon it. Jesus said, Take ye away the stone. Martha, the sister of him that was dead, saith unto him, Lord, by this time he stinketh: for he has been dead four days. Jesus saith unto her, Said I not unto thee, that, if thou wouldest believe, thou shouldest see the glory of God? Then they took away the stone from the place where the dead was laid. And Jesus lifted up his eyes, and said, Father, I thank thee that thou hast heard me. And I knew that thou hearest me always: but because of the people which stand by I said it, that they may believe that thou hast sent me.

In the last lecture, we considered briefly, these wonderful words, *Jesus wept*. When he saw Mary weeping, and the Jews weeping, he groaned within himself, and said, 'Where have ye laid him?' They said, 'Come and see.' And as they led him along the path to the cave in the rock, 'Jesus wept.' Amazing sight! 'Jesus wept.' He was the Son of God, who thought it no robbery to be equal with God, infinite in happiness, and yet he weeps, so truly does he feel the sorrows of his own.

(1) The feelings of the Jews at this sight

Wonder at his love. 'Behold how he loved him!'

These Jews were as yet only worldly men, and yet they were amazed at such an overflow of love. They saw that heavenly form bowed down at the grave of Lazarus, they heard his groans of agony, they saw the tears that fell like rain from his compassionate eyes, they saw the heaving of his seamless mantle. But, ah! they saw not what was within. They saw but a little of his love, they did not see its eternity. They did not see that it was love that made him die for Lazarus. They did not know the fullness, freeness, vastness of that love of his.

And yet they were astonished at it. 'Behold how he loved him!' There is something in the love of Christ to amaze even worldly men.

When Jesus gives peace to his own in the midst of trouble, when the waves of trouble come round the soul, when clouds and darkness, poverty and distress overwhelm his dwelling, when he can yet be glad in the Lord, and say: 'Although the fig-tree shall not blossom, neither shall fruit be in the vines; the labour of the olive shall fail, and the fields shall yield no meat; the flock shall be cut off from the fold, and there shall be no herd in the stalls: yet I will rejoice in the Lord, I will joy in the God of my salvation'; then the world are forced to say, 'Behold how he loved him!'

When Jesus is with the believer in death, standing beside him so that he cannot be moved, overshadowing him with his wings, washing him in his blood, and filling him with holy peace, so that he cries, 'To depart, and be with Christ, is far better,' then the world cry, 'Behold how he loved him!' 'Let me die the death of the righteous, and let my last end be like his!'

Another solemn day is coming when all of you who are believers shall be separated, and stand on the right hand of the throne, and

Jesus shall welcome you, poor and hell-deserving though you be, to share his throne, and to share his glory. Then you who are unbelievers shall cry, with bitter wailing, 'Behold how he loved them!'

Some doubt his love
'Could not this man, which opened the eyes of the blind, have caused that even this man should not have died?' (v. 37). It was but a little before that Jesus had given sight to a man that was born blind; and the Jews that now stood around had seen the miracle. Now they reasoned thus with one another: If he really loved Lazarus, could he not have kept him from dying? He that opened the eyes of the blind, could also preserve the dying from

death. They doubted his tears, they doubted his words. This is unbelief. It turns aside the plainest declarations of the Lord Jesus by its own arguments. How many of you have turned aside the love of Christ in the same way!

We read that he wept over Jerusalem. This plainly showed that he did not want them to die in their sins – that he does not want you to perish, but to have everlasting life. And yet you doubt his love, and turn aside his tears by some wretched argument of your own. Jesus says: 'Come unto me, all ye that labour, and are heavy laden, and I will give you rest.' This is a simple declaration, but you turn it aside thus: If Christ had really wanted to give me rest, would he not have brought me to himself before now? Unbelief turns the very exhibition of Christ's love into gall and wormwood. Some men, the more they see of Christ, the harder they grow. These Jews had seen him give sight to the blind, and weep over Lazarus, and yet they only grew harder. Take heed that it be not so with you. Take heed lest the more you hear of Christ, and of his love to his own, the harder you grow.

(2) The scene at the grave
The command: 'Take ye away the stone'
Christ's ways are not as our ways, nor his thoughts like our thoughts. One would have thought that he would have commanded the stone

to fly back by his own word.

When he rose from the dead himself, 'the angel of the Lord descended from heaven, and came and rolled back the stone from the door and sat upon it'; but he did not do so now. He said to the men, 'Take ye away the stone' for two reasons. First, he wanted to bring out Martha's unbelief, that it might be made manifest. Unbelief in the heart is like evil humour in a wound – it festers; and therefore Jesus wanted to draw it out of Martha's heart. Second, to teach us to use the means. The men around the grave could not give life to dead Lazarus, but they could roll back the stone. Now Jesus was about to use his divine power in awaking the dead, but he would not take away the stone.

Have any of you an unconverted friend for whom you pray? You know it is only Christ that can give him life, it is only Christ that can call him forth. Yet you can roll away the stone – you can use the means, you can bring your friend under the faithful preaching of the gospel. Speak to him, write to him. 'Take away the stone.'

Martha's unbelief: 'Lord, by this time he stinketh, for he hath been dead four days'

Mary was silent. She did not know what Jesus was going to do; but she knew that he would do all things well. She knew that he was full of love and wisdom and grace. But Martha cries out. She forgot all the words of Christ. She forgot his message: 'This sickness is not unto death, but for the glory of God, that the Son of God may be glorified thereby.' She forgot his sweet saying, 'Thy brother shall rise again' and 'I am the resurrection and the life; he that believeth on me, though he were dead, yet shall he live.' She forgot her own declaration that Jesus was the Son of God. And see how she would have hindered her own mercy. She loved her brother tenderly, and yet she would have the stone kept on the mouth of the cave. She was standing in her own light.

Learn how easily you may fall into unbelief. A few minutes before, Martha was full of faith; but now she sinks again. Oh, what marvellous blindness and sin there is in the human heart!

Learn how unbelief shuts out your own mercy. 'He did not many mighty works there, because of their unbelief.' Martha had nearly hindered the restoration of Lazarus. Oh, do not forget the words of Jesus, nor his wonders of love and power! 'Is anything too hard for the Lord?'

Christ's reproof: 'Said I not unto thee, that if thou wouldest believe, thou shouldest see the glory of God?' (v. 40)

Christ had sent this message: 'This sickness is not unto death'; now he recalls his word: 'Said I not unto thee?' as if he had said, Martha, have you forgotten my words? Am I a liar, or like waters that fail? Am

I a man that I should lie, or the son of man that I should repent? See how unbelief wounded Jesus. 'He that believeth not God, hath made him a liar.' You will have a deeper hell than the heathen. They will be cast away because of their sins, but you because of your sin and unbelief. 'He that believeth not is condemned already.'

(3) Christ's prayer and thanksgiving

His prayer was secret

We are not told any words that he prayed; but no doubt during his groans and tears he was praying to his Father in secret. Even in the midst of the crowd, Jesus was alone with his Father, praying for his own that their faith might not fail. The tears of Christ were not mere tears of feeling, they were the tears also of earnest prayer. His is no empty fellow-feeling, but real intercession. Christ teaches you to pray in sudden trials. Even when you cannot get any secret place, lift up your heart to him in the midst of the crowd. Ah, brethren! a sincere soul is never at a loss for a praying place to meet with God.

If you are a child of God, you will find some secret place to pray. It will not do to say, you will pray when walking, or at your work, or in the midst of company. It will not do to make that your praying time through the day. No; Satan is at your right hand. Get alone with God. Spend as much time as you can alone with God every day; and then, in sudden temptations and afflictions, you will be able to lift your heart easily even among the crowd to your Father's ear.

His thanksgiving
'Father, I thank thee that thou hast heard me, and I knew that thou hearest me always; but because of the people which stand by I said it, that they may believe that thou hast sent me.'

See what *speed* Christ comes in his prayer: 'Thou hearest me always.' Every intercession that Christ makes is answered. The moment he asks he is answered. If we know that Christ prays for us, then we know that we have what he desires.

He *thanks*. So entirely one is

Christ with his own, that he gives thanks in our name. This should teach us not only to pray, but also to give thanks.

He does this *aloud*, that all around might believe on him. Christ was always seeking the conversion of souls, even here, in praying and giving thanks to his Father. He does it aloud, that those around him might believe on him, as the sent of God, and the Saviour of the world. Yea, brethren, he records it here, that ye may believe on him. For this end is Christ set before you in the gospel as the sent of God, the compassionate Saviour, the Mediator and Intercessor, that ye may believe on him.

SEVEN

John 11: 43-46

And when he thus had spoken, he cried with a loud voice, Lazarus, come forth. And he that was dead came forth, bound hand and foot with grave clothes: and his face was bound about with a napkin, Jesus saith unto them, Loose him, and let him go. Then many of the Jews which came to Mary, and had seen the things which Jesus did, believed on him. But some of them went their ways to the Pharisees, and told them what things Jesus had done.

(1) The raising of dead Lazarus

The time: 'When he thus had spoken'

When Jesus first heard that Lazarus was sick, he abode two days in the place where he was. Slowly and calmly he moved toward Bethany, so that when he arrived beneath its fig-trees, the passing villager told him that Lazarus had lain in the grave four days already.

Still Jesus did not hurry, but waited till he had drawn forth the unbelief of Martha and Mary, waited till he had manifested his own tender, compassionate heart, waited till he had given public thanks to the Father to show that he was sent of God. 'And when he thus had spoken, he cried with a loud voice,

Lazarus, come forth.'

His time is the right time. So will it be in giving life to Israel. Israel, like Lazarus, have been lying in their graves eighteen hundred years. Their bones are dry and very many. Since he spake against them, he earnestly remembers them still; and there is a day coming when he will pour the Spirit of life upon them, and make them come forth, and be life to the dead world. But this in his own time.

Jesus does not hurry. He waits till he has drawn out the unbelief of men, and manifested his own tender heart. Then when his time is come, he will cry, Israel, come forth. So in the deliverance of the church; so in the deliverance of individual believers: 'For yet a little while, and he that shall come will come, and will not tarry.'

The work: 'He cried with a loud voice, Lazarus, come forth.' And he that was dead came forth, bound hand and foot with grave-clothes.'

What a strange scene was here! It was a retired part of the narrow ravine in which Bethany lies, and the crowd were standing beside the newly-opened sepulchre of Lazarus. It was a cave cut in the rock, and the huge stone that had been rolled to the door was now rolled back. The Jews stood around, wondering what he would do. The hardy peasants of Bethany leaned over the newly-moved stone and gazed into the dark cave. Martha and Mary fixed their eyes on Jesus, and a deep silence hung upon the group. Opposite the cavern's mouth stood the Saviour, his tears not yet dried, his eye looking up towards his Father. 'He cried with a loud voice, Lazarus, come forth!' The hollow cave rang with the solemn sound.

The ear of Lazarus was dead and cold, the limbs stiff and motionless, the eyelids closely sealed, and the cold damp of death lay on his forehead; the grave-clothes were round him, and his face bound with a napkin, when the sudden cry, 'Lazarus, come forth,' awoke the dead. It pierced down into the deep cave, and through the close damp napkin into the dead ear. The heart began suddenly to beat, and the warm current of life to flow through the dead man's veins. The vital heat and the sense of hearing came back. It was a well-known voice. 'The voice of my Beloved,' he would say, 'he calls my name.' So he arose: 'And he that was dead came forth, bound hand and foot, with grave-clothes.'

How simple, and yet how glorious! Jehovah speaks, and it is done. 'The voice of the Lord is powerful, the voice of the Lord is full of majesty; the voice of the Lord breaketh the cedars, yea, the Lord breaketh the cedars of Lebanon.' Now were the words of Christ fulfilled: 'This sickness is not unto death, but for the glory of God, that the Son of God may be glorified thereby.' Christ manifested forth his glory as the resurrection and the life.

(2) The resurrection

This is the way in which Christ will raise all that have died in the Lord. 'Marvel not at this: for the hour is coming, in which all that are in their graves shall hear his voice, and shall come forth; they that have done good, unto the resurrection of life; and they that have done evil, unto the resurrection of damnation' (John 5:28, 29). There is a day near at hand, in which every dead ear shall hear the same voice crying, Come forth! Come forth!

Learn not to sorrow over departed believers as those who have no hope: 'For if we believe that Jesus died and rose again, even so them also that sleep in Jesus will God bring with him.' The dust of Lazarus was dear to Jesus; he would not leave it in the rocky tomb. So is the dust of every Lazarus dear in his sight. He will not lose so much as one of them. Wherever they lie, it matters not – beneath the deep blue sea, or on some distant battlefield, or consumed in flame and smoke – the Lord Jesus will yet collect their scattered dust, and make them like his own glorious body.

Learn not to fear the grave. There is nothing that we naturally shrink back from more than the grave. Ah! it is a fearful thing to leave the company of living men, and lie down in the narrow house, with a shroud for our only clothing, a coffin for our couch, and the worm for our companion. It is humiliating, it is loathsome. But if you are one of Christ's, here is the victory: 'In a moment, in the twinkling of an eye, at the last trump: for the trumpet shall sound, and the dead shall be raised incorruptible, and we shall be changed. For this corruptible must put on incorruption, and this mortal must put on immortality. So when this corruptible shall have put on incorruption, and this mortal shall have put on immortality, then shall be brought to pass the saying that is written, Death is swallowed up in victory. O death, where is thy sting? O grave, where is thy victory?' (1 Cor. 15:52-55).

Fix your eye on Jesus at the grave of Lazarus; so will he stand over the grave of a sleeping world, and cry, 'Come forth!'

O Christless man! you too will hear that voice. Your soul will hear it in hell, your body will hear it in the grave; and death and hell will give up the dead which are in them. You will not hear his voice now, but you must hear it then. You will come forth, like Lazarus, and stand before God. Perhaps you would like to lie still in the grave. Oh! let the rocks fall on me, and the mountains cover me. Perhaps you will cling to the sides of the grave, and clasp your frail coffin in your arms. Perhaps your soul would wish to lie still in hell. Oh! let me alone! Let the burning wave go over for ever, let the worm gnaw and never die. But you must come forth to the resurrection of damnation. You must rise to shame and everlasting contempt.

(3) The life

This is the way in which Christ gives life to dead souls. 'Verily, verily, I say unto you, The hour is coming, and now is, when the dead shall hear the voice of the Son of God: and they that hear shall live' (John 5:25).

The soul of the unconverted among you is as dead to divine things as the body of Lazarus was to common things. There is a total death in every unconverted bosom. It is not a mere figure of speech. It is not figurative death, but real – as real as that of Lazarus. Your eye does not see divine things, your ear does not hear them, your heart does not feel them.

It is the voice of Christ that wakens

the dead soul. Jesus speaks through the Bible, through ministers, through providences. His voice can reach the dead. He quickeneth whom he will. They that hear, live.

Learn that it is right in ministers and godly friends to give warnings, and calls, and invitations to those that are spiritually dead. It appears strange to some that we should believe men to be spiritually dead, and yet warn them, and call them, and invite them to repent and believe the gospel. But this is the very way Jesus did to a dead Lazarus; and the way he does still to dead souls. It is through these very warnings, and calls, and invitations that Jesus speaks to your dead hearts. All that have been saved in this place heard the voice of Christ when they were dead. Godly persons among you should continue these calls and warnings, even though your friends appear as dead as Lazarus was.

Learn where to look for spiritual life. It was not the voice of Mary, nor the voice of Martha, nor the voice of the Jews that raised dead Lazarus. They could roll away the stone, but they could do no more. They could not raise the dead. It was the voice of Immanuel – of him who is the life of all that live. So it is still, dear friends. It is his voice alone that can awaken you. It is not my voice, nor that of your loving Marthas and Marys – it must be the voice of Jesus, or you will sleep on and die in your sins, and where Christ has gone you will never come. Many a time the voice of ministers has rung through this house, and through your ears, and you have lived on in sin. But when the voice of Christ speaks through the Word, then you will arise, and leave all, and follow him.

(4) The effect on the bystanders
Many believed on him
It was a happy day in Bethany. He turneth the shadow of death into the morning. Martha and Mary had their bitter grief turned into a song of praise. Their buried brother was once more restored to their arms safe and sound; and I can imagine the feelings with which they sang that evening at their family worship: 'Return unto thy rest, O my soul, for

the Lord had dealt bountifully with thee.'

Another joy was this: all their unbelief was now cleared away; Christ was like a morning without clouds. His tarrying, his promise, his trial of them – all was now explained; and as Mary sat at his feet that evening and heard his words, she felt more than ever that it was impossible for Christ to lie.

But a greater joy still remained: 'Many of the Jews believed on him.' It was a birth-night for eternity. The Shepherd found some lost sheep that night. The voice that called Lazarus forth pierced many a heart. The cottage at Bethany would be like a little heaven that night.

Observe what made them believe: 'When they saw the things that

Jesus did.' It was not the sight of one thing, but of all that Jesus did. Just as the dying thief believed on Christ, not from seeing one thing but all that Jesus did. When he saw his holy person, his calmness, his love, his pity, he could not but feel that this was the Son of God, and the Saviour of the world. So with these Jews. They saw the amazing love of Jesus to Lazarus, and Martha and Mary; they saw his tears, they heard his groans, they saw him thank and praise his Father; and they could not but believe on him.

Two things especially they saw: divine power and divine love to sinners. It is the same thing which persuades sinners now to believe on him. It is seeing such love in him that he is willing to save; and such power that he is able.

And O how happy it would make us if many of you believed on him! If you were constrained this day to lay hold on him as your surety, elder brother and friend!

Some went and told the Pharisees
Some were saved and some were hardened.

Their companions were saved, yet they were not. They left Jerusalem together, strangers to God and to conversion. Some were taken, and some were left. So it is ever. I have often thought when sinners have been stricken and saved in this place, surely their neighbours will be saved also. Often it is the very reverse. Are there not many of you that have been hardened, while others have been saved by your side?

They loved Martha and Mary, and yet were not saved, but hated Christ. They were friends of Martha and Mary; they seem even to have loved Mary best, and yet they did not love Christ. So it is now. Some among you love our Marthas and Marys, and yet do not love Christ. Ah! those whom you love will soon be eternally separated from you.

Their objections were answered, and yet they were not saved. 'Could not this man who opened the eyes of the blind, have caused that even this man should not have died?' They objected that his love was not true, or he would not have suffered Lazarus to drop into the grave. Here their objection is taken away. Lazarus is raised, so that it is proved to them that Jesus loved him. Their mouth is shut. Still they do not turn. Alas! it is the same still. Many say, If I knew that Christ was willing to receive me, I would come. Remove the objection, still they do not come. If I had clothes, if I were free from family cares, I would begin to care about my soul. Still, remove the objection, and they are as careless as ever.

They hated Christ, the more they saw of him. Not only did they not believe on him, but they went and told his deadly enemies, they went and plotted his destruction. Ah! this is almost incredible. What a diabolical heart is a natural heart! Not only do you refuse to be saved by Christ, but you hate his name and cause. 'Behold, I lay in Zion a stumbling-stone and rock of offence; and whosoever believeth on him shall not be ashamed.'